TO
OUR NECKS OF KIN
(blood relatives)
Aron
Eden
Hope
Lee

"I give up, Lois, what has sharp teeth, bad breath and blood on his cape?"

"Happy Wooden Anniversary, dear."

VAMPIRE JOKES AND CARTOONS

"A Comedy of Terrors"

Edited by Phil Hirsch and Paul Laikin

PYRAMID BOOKS NEW YORK

VAMPIRE JOKES AND CARTOONS
"A Comedy of Terrors"

First edition published September, 1974.

ISBN 0-515-03498-3
Library of Congress Catalog Card Number: 74-5605
Printed in the United States of America

Pyramid Books are published by Pyramid Communications, Inc. Its trademarks, consisting of the word "Pyramid" and the portrayal of a pyramid, are registered in the United States Patent Office.

Pyramid Communications, Inc., 919 Third Avenue,
New York, N.Y. 10022

A PYRAMID BOOK

What happens when vampires get together?

They drive each other bats!

Why did the vampire pass Mick Jagger by?

You can't get blood out of a Stone!

What is the motto of the Vampires of America, Incorporated?

A Fiend in Need Is a Fiend in Deed!

LEMONADE
3 cents
per
GLASS

BLOOD
3 cents
PER
SIP
EDWING

What did the vampire do when the panhandler stopped him and said he hadn't had a bite in days?

He bit him!

Why don't vampires ever go after heavy girls?

They like something in a lighter vein!

What kind of first aid do vampires give?

Mouth-to-neck resuscitation!

"Quick, operator, how do I Dial-a-Prayer?"

A TRANSYLVANIAN KNOCK-KNOCK JOKE

Knock, Knock!

Who's there?

Ivan!

Ivan who?

Ivan to drink your blood!

"Hey, Nancy, your blind date is here."

"Your diabetic victims are giving you cavities."

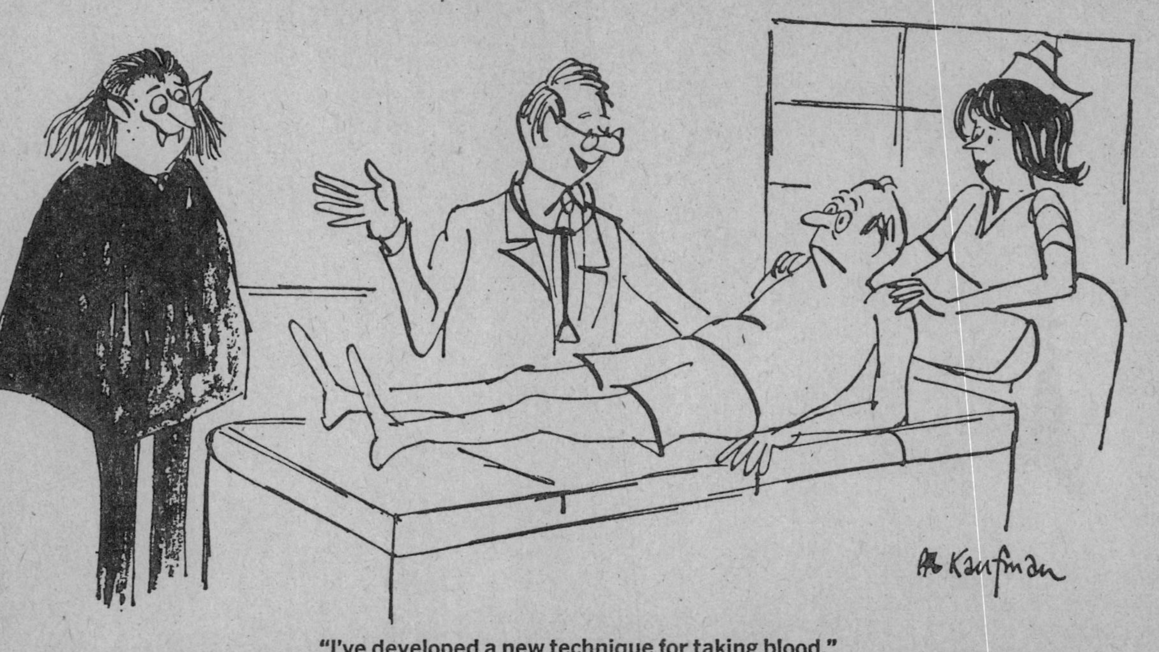

"I've developed a new technique for taking blood."

CITY TOW
EDWING

Where do wealthy vampires keep their valuables hidden?

In Swiss blood banks!

When does a vampire go to a blood bank?

When he wants to make a withdrawal.

What was the vampire doing driving on the turnpike?

Looking for the main artery!

"Nonsense—I always make house calls."

How do you kill a hungry vampire?

You drive a steak through his heart!

Where can you buy a vampire?

At a monster sale!

What is the vampires' favorite song?

"Moonlight Becomes You."

"Blood! Blood!"

"Oh, it's only you. I thought for a moment it was my teacher."

What do you feed a 500-pound vampire?

Anything it wants!

Why do vampires like comedians?

They like things in a jocular vein!

"I'm sorry, sir, but we don't get many calls for body snatchers."

Where do vampires stay when they are in the New York City area?

Great Neck!

What do country vampires wear?

Seer-sucker suits!

What happens in a vampire horse race?

They finish neck and neck!

How do you spot a vampire jockey?

He always wins by a neck!

What is the theme song of the Vampires of America?

When the Moon Comes Over the Mountain!

What happens when a vampire attends a vaudeville show?

He goes for the juggler!

FREE
BLOOD
TEST!
REGISTER HERE.

"It was okay until the vampire and the lady ghoul started getting mushy."

"Dear Sirs: In reference to your letter . . . Relax, a parade is going by."

EDWING

"Darn blood clots!"

THE TOP TV SHOWS FROM TRANSYLVANIA

TOOTH OR CONSEQUENCES

WEIRD WEIRD WORLD

LUMP UNTO MY FEET

continued

BAT-MAN

LOVE TRANSYLVANIAN STYLE

HOWL IN THE FAMILY

LITTLE SCIENTIST

"Sniff . . . sniff . . . sniff . . ."

What does a vampire do when the moon doesn't come out?

Hangs around the house!

What does a vampire say to his girlfriend?

"Let's neck!"

What advice did the father vampire give his teen-age son?

Always bite the hand that feeds you!

"If you see the Tooth Fairy around, will you tell him that I've got a wiggly front tooth?"

What's a vampire's favorite drink?

A Bloody Mary!

What do they shout at Transylvanian baseball games?

"Kill The Vampire! Kill The Vampire!"

Where is a sucker born every minute?

In Transylvania!

EDWING

TOYS

BLOOD BANK
TYPES OF BLO

"Gee, this is the latest I've ever stayed out on a date—
do you realize it's almost sunrise?"

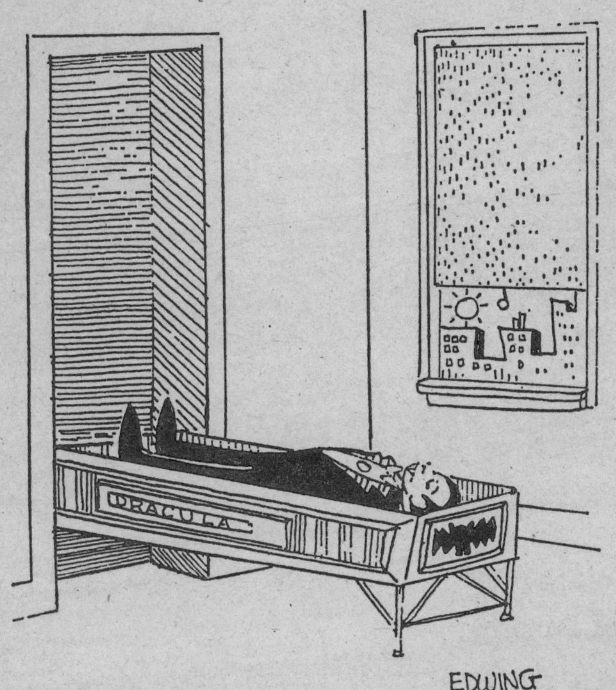
DRACULA
EDWING

When is a vampire on the ball?

When he turns into a bat!

What do vampire panhandlers do?

Put the bite on people!

What is the national anthem of the Vampires of America?

"*Fangs for the Memory!*"

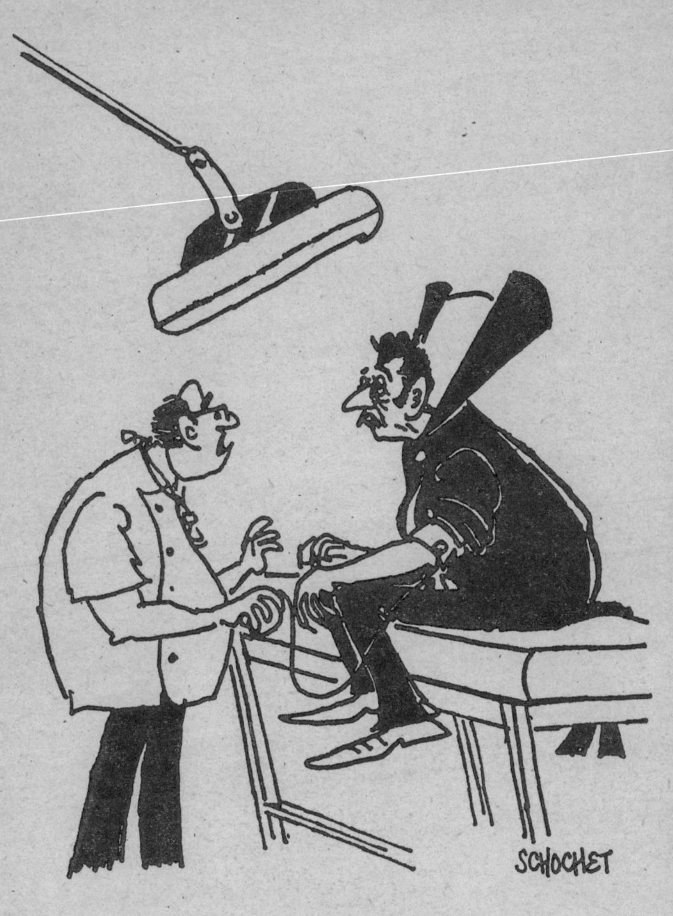

"You have to be very careful these days. There's a lot of tired blood going around."

"Darn those pesky little bloodsuckers!"

"I knew there'd be bats in the Cooperstown caves."

"Care to join me in a bite?"

"LIsten, are you certain you can put me up for the night? . . . I mean, I don't want to impose . . . "

Why aren't vampires good gamblers?

They're always making sucker bets!

What did the Godfather do when the vampire refused his offer?

He put the head of an albino in his bed!

Why are vampires insane?

Because they have bats in the belfry!

"Would you care to lie down and see how it feels?"

"I think it's time for Junior to have a little brother or sister."

"... and for those of you who cannot give cash, I hope you will lend me your immoral support."

Why did the vampire dig for gold?

He wanted to strike a rich vein!

How does a vampire aggravate a person?

He eats his heart out!

Why do vampires avoid mountain areas?

Because you can't get blood out of a stone!

"Drat . . . I forgot my doggie bag!"

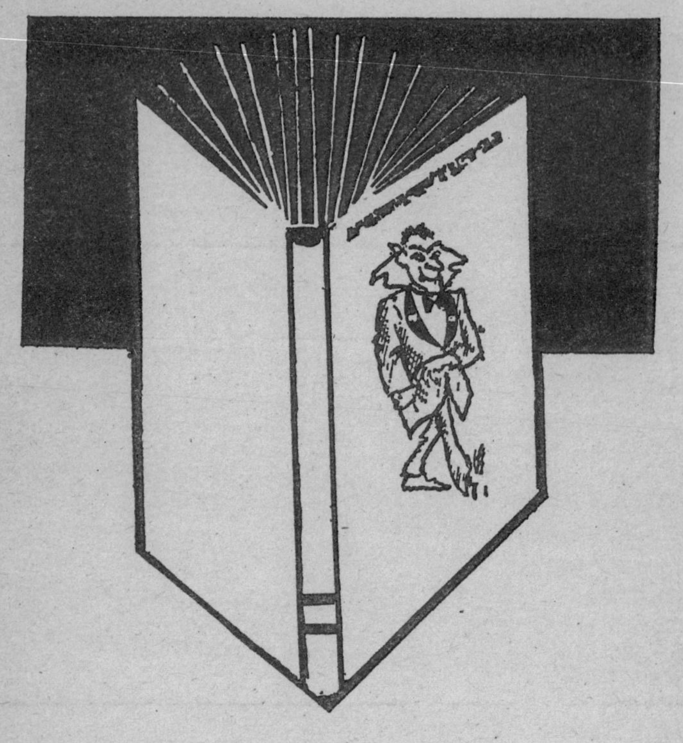

BEST-SELLING
VAMPIRE
BOOKS

EVERYTHING YOU ALWAYS WANTED TO KNOW ABOUT NECKS (BUT WERE AFRAID TO ASK)

YOU ARE WHAT YOU EAT

IN OLD BLOOD

continued

THE MOON AND SIX-PINTS

OF HUMAN BANDAGE

FROM BIER TO ETERNITY

"Sorry, sir, this vampire book you wrote lacks realism."

What kind of clerical work do vampires do?

They file their teeth!

Why do vampires hang around with their own kind?

Because blood is thicker than water!

Where do you usually find vampires?

In any neck of the woods!

"Look, kid, I told you—collecting trash is no picnic in Transylvania."

What's the worst ailment a vampire faces?

A stiff neck!

Why can't a vampire ever get justice?

Because people never give a sucker an even break!

How does a vampire make a living?

He moonlights!

"... Then the vampire, bless his soul, drank heartily of Snow White, Jack and Jill, Little Miss Muffet, Mary and her little lamb and Little Boy Blue ... and lived happily ever after."

TOP TEN
VAMPIRE
SONGS

FULL MOON AND EMPTY ARMS

GHOUL OF MY DREAMS

FANGS FOR THE MEMORY

PEG IN MY HEART

continued

BY THE TIME I GET TO V-NECKS

I LEFT MY HEART IN TRANSYLVANIA

I AIN'T GOT NOBODY

I'LL BE SEIZING YOU
(IN ALL THE OLD FAMILIAR PLACES)

THE BIRTH OF THE BRUISE

I WONDER WHO'S KISSING HER NECK

EDWING

"Tell me, my dear, do you know any drinking songs?"

SCHOCHET

"We're overdrawn again at the blood bank."

ALL-TIME
GREAT
VAMPIRE MOVIES

IT HAPPENED ONE BITE

THE BEST BIERS OF OUR LIVES

A SCAR IS BORN

GRIEF ENCOUNTER

SUNDAY, BLOODY SUNDAY!

SEVEN BITES FOR SEVEN BROTHERS

CAPE FEAR

"Oh, good—another comedy."

"Just the newspaper, Hugo. Put back the newsboy!"

1
3
5

2
4
6
SCHUCHET

What does a vampire usually borrow from his neighbor?

A cup of blood!

Why aren't vampires good gamblers?

They're always making sucker bets!

What is the vampires' favorite drinking toast?

Here's blood in your eye!

"It's about this $10,000 deduction for blood money . . ."

"You don't photograph too well!"

"Wow! It sure doesn't taste like tomato juice!"

"I think my mother is getting suspicious. She wonders where all the Bloody Marys are going.

FOR THE VAMPIRE WHO HAS EVERYTHING

Handy Little Home Blood Bank: Set something aside for a sunny day. Don't bother to go out moonlighting. Stay home some rainy nights and sip away in the comfort of your own casket. Ideal for late-night withdrawals.

Bullet-Proof Cape: Prevents stakes from entering the heart. What's more, it is completely washable. Gets out those deep, deep blood stains, and no matter what laundry soap is used, it comes out blacker than black. Ideal if you want to paint the town red.

Set of False Fangs: If you haven't been as sharp as you'd like to be, try these and you will sharpen your potential. Something you can really dig your teeth into, especially if you are getting old and your bark is worse than your bite. Specify if you want it complete—with dripping saliva.

Road Map of Transylvania and Points East, West, North and South: Follow the major (and minor) arteries to favorite dining out spots. Now you can get back to the old haunt, repose satiated in your coffin before the sun comes up. Ideal if a sudden thirst makes you want one for the road.

CORRESPONDENCE SCHOOL FOR VAMPIRES: Even a high school dropout can learn how to put the bite on people at the Bloodsucker School for Vampires, situated right in the heart of downtown Eerie, Transylvania. Courses in how not to leave a hickey; what to do when you get a stiff neck; how to really go bats, and 101 things to do if the full moon doesn't come out. Correspondence courses approved by the G.I. Bill (Ghouls, Inc.). Just send us your blood sample. People are dying for our graduates' attention, and Hollywood is clamoring to give our students roles in horror films.

"I'm pooped. I must have gotten some tired blood tonight."

"Nothing to get excited about. Probably just another guy on his way to *Let's Make a Deal.*"

What animal do vampires like best?

The giraffe!

Why is General Patton a vampire hero?

He was all blood and guts!

When does a vampire have a bad day?

When he gets up on the wrong side of the coffin!

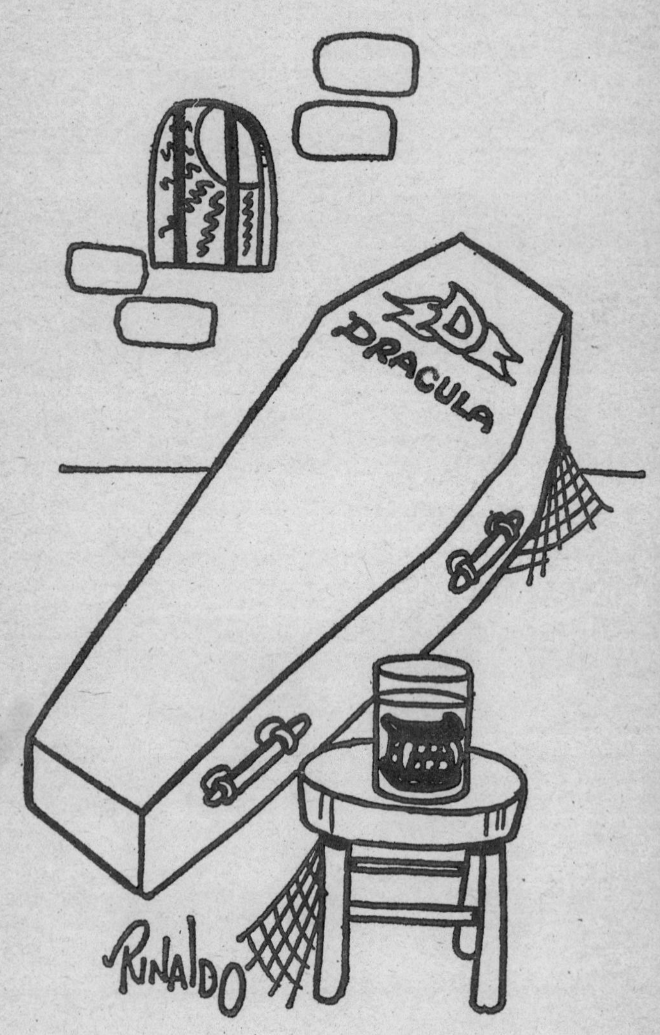
D
DRACULA
RINALDO